THE JAGUAR

THE BIG CAT DISCOVERY LIBRARY

Lynn M. Stone

Rourke Enterprises, Inc.
Vero Beach, Florida 32964

PHOTO CREDITS
© Lynn M. Stone: Pages 1, 4, 7, 8, 12, 13, 15, 18, 21, and cover;
© C. Allan Morgan/DRK Photo: Page 10; © Zib Leszczynski/
Animals Animals: Page 17

ACKNOWLEDGEMENTS

The author wishes to thank the following for photographic
assistance in the preparation of this book: Nancy Tetzlaf
and Jungle Larry's Safari, Naples, Fla.

Library of Congress Cataloging-in-Publication Date
Stone, Lynn M.
    Jaguars / Lynn M. Stone.
    p. cm. — (The big cat discovery library)
    Includes index.
    Summary: An introduction to the physical characteristics,
habits, natural environment, relationship to humans, and
future of the jaguar, the biggest wild cat in the Americas.
    ISBN 0-86592-506-2
    1. Jaguars—Juvenile literature [1. Jaguars.] I. Title.
II. Series: Stone, Lynn M. Big cat discovery library.
QL737.C23S768 1989   89-32646
599.74'428—dc20   CIP
                       AC

TABLE OF CONTENTS

THE JAGUAR

In 1500 the explorer Amerigo Vespucci thought he had found leopards in South America. Vespucci had found big, spotted cats. As it turned out, they were not leopards.

Other European explorers began calling the spotted cats "el tigre." Yet the cats weren't tigers either.

The explorer had actually discovered jaguars *(Panthera onca),* the biggest wild cats in the Americas. The word "jaguar" came from the language of a South American Indian tribe. Spanish-speaking Americans, however, still call the jaguar "el tigre".

Whatever it is called, the jaguar is one of the great meat-eating animals of the world.

THE JAGUAR'S COUSINS

The jaguar's cousins are the cats. Like its cousins, the jaguar has typical cat, or **feline**, looks and habits. Its claws, teeth, blunt snout, hunting methods, and flexible body are those of a cat.

The jaguar's closest cousin is the leopard. Leopards, too, are spotted and have similar bodies to jaguars.

Jaguars are also closely related to tigers and lions. All of these cats—leopards, tigers, lions, and jaguars—make deep, coughing noises called roars.

Several slightly different types of jaguars exist. Some jaguars in Brazil and Argentina, for instance, are much larger than the jaguars of Central America.

HOW THEY LOOK

Jaguars and leopards are difficult to tell apart. Jaguars, however, look stockier than leopards. A jaguar has a very muscular body, a thick neck, and short, stout legs.

A jaguar's spots are somewhat circular with a black dot inside the circle. These spots are called **rosettes**. Circle spots on leopards don't usually have a dot inside the ring.

Just as black leopards are fairly common, so are black jaguars. Black-furred jaguars are usually found in the dark, wet forests of Brazil and Paraguay.

A male jaguar weighs from 120 to 200 pounds. One record-sized male weighed 350 pounds. Females average 80 to 100 pounds.

Jaguar Fur

WHERE THEY LIVE

Jaguars live throughout much of South America, Central America, and Mexico. Jaguars used to live in small numbers in Arizona, New Mexico, southern California, and Texas. Now it is extremely unusual for a jaguar to be seen anywhere north of Mexico.

The jaguar's favorite home, or **habitat**, is a dark, wet, tropical forest. If the forest has a river or swamp, so much the better.

Yet jaguars have also been found in the mountains of Peru and Bolivia up to 8,860 feet. The jaguars of western Mexico and the southwestern United States live in desert conditions!

Jaguar in Tree

Black Jaguar

Black Jaguar

HOW THEY LIVE

Being cats, jaguars spend much of their lives resting. They also take time to sharpen their claws and groom themselves with their long, rough tongues.

Because they live in warm climates, jaguars cool off in streams and ponds. They are excellent swimmers. They like the water even more than Bengal tigers do.

Normally, jaguars walk. But they are fast afoot when they need to be.

Jaguars usually travel and hunt alone, except for females with cubs.

Old and very young male jaguars may roam over several hundred square miles. Most other males stick to a personal home range called a **territory**.

Jaguar Growling

THE JAGUAR'S CUBS

Baby jaguars may be born at any time in South America. In northern jaguar country, the cubs are usually born in the summer.

A typical jaguar **litter** has one to four cubs. They are born in the shelter of bushes, rocks, or trees.

Jaguar cubs begin to grow up on their mother's milk and on meat that she brings to them. The cubs trail their mother when they are just six weeks old. Several months pass before they do any hunting on their own. Jaguars probably stay with their mother for up to two years.

Captive jaguars have lived into their early twenties.

PREDATOR AND PREY

Throughout its home range, the jaguar is the most powerful **predator**, or hunter. It hunts by ambushing or **stalking** other animals, its **prey**. Most jaguars hunt at night. Like other big cats, jaguars have excellent vision and hearing.

Usually a jaguar hunts on the ground and creeps almost like a snake toward its prey. But jaguars will climb trees for sloths and splash into water for fish and other creatures.

For its size, the jaguar may have the most powerful jaws of any cat. Jaguars often kill by biting through their victim's skull.

Jaguars can kill large animals, like tapirs, which they hide for later meals. They also kill such small animals as turkeys, armadillos, and turtles.

Jaguar Prey: Brazilian Tapir

JAGUARS AND PEOPLE

For centuries, jaguars have been extremely important to the native people of South and Central America. Jaguars have been both feared and respected. Some early South American Indians thought jaguars were gods. One tribe carved 20-ton statues of jaguars. Jaguars have been the topics of countless legends.

Although feared by people, jaguars have rarely attacked humans. In fact, many South American Indians used to raise jaguars as family pets.

Many jaguars were killed in the 1960s and 1970s when the fur of spotted cats was in great demand.

Jaguars can usually be found in zoos. Captives do not produce cubs as often as lion and tiger captives do.

Black Jaguar

THE JAGUAR'S FUTURE

The trade in jaguar fur has been slowed. South American countries have begun to protect their "tigres." In 1984, Belize, a country in Central America, opened the first park in the world just for the safety of jaguars.

The jaguar is **endangered** in many other places, though. Angry farmers kill jaguars for attacking their cattle and sheep. **Poachers**, people who hunt against the law, still shoot a few jaguars. Worse, jaguars are losing their land. Huge sections of green jungle are being burned and bulldozed for farms and villages in South America.

If more countries do not follow the lead of Belize, wild jaguars will continue to disappear.

Glossary

endangered (en DANE jerd)—in danger of no longer existing; very rare

feline (FEE line)—any of the cats

habitat (HAB a tat)—the area in which an animal lives

litter (LIT er)—a group of baby animals born of the same mother at the same time

poacher (PO cher)—someone who hunts animals when it is against the law

predator (PRED a tor)—an animal that kills other animals for food

prey (PRAY)—an animal that is hunted for food by another animal

rosette (ro ZET)—a spot or group of spots that look similar to a flower

territory (TER rih tory)—a home area defended by certain animals that live within it

stalk (STAWK)—hunting by moving slowly and quietly toward prey

INDEX